T0049078

ULTIMATE ADVENTURE SPORTS
MOUNTAIN BIKING
- EXCLUSIVE -

AUTHOR

SALLY WARREN

First Published 2023
by Redback Publishing

PO Box 357, Frenchs Forest, NSW 2086, Australia

www.redbackpublishing.com
orders@redbackpublishing.com

© Redback Publishing 2023

ISBN 978-1-922322-98-2 HBK

All rights reserved. No part of this publication may be reproduced in any form or by
any means (including photocopying or storing it in any medium by electronic means
and whether or not transiently or incidentally to some other use of this publication)
without the written permission of the copyright owner. Applications for the copyright
owner's written permission should be addressed to the publisher.

Author: Sally Warren
Editor: Caroline Thomas
Designer: Redback Publishing

Original illustrations:
© Redback Publishing 2023
Originated by Redback Publishing

Printed and bound in Malaysia

Acknowledgements
Abbreviations: l—left, r—right, b—bottom, t—top,
c—centre, m—middle
We would like to thank the following for permission to reproduce photographs:
(Images © Shutterstock) p6bl Clunkers original mtn bikes Charlie Kelly via http://
www.sonic.net/~ckelly/Seekay/index.htm#kelly_family, p6br 1984 Alba Vasconcelos
via Wikimedia Commons, p7tl by Camerasandcoffee/Shutterstock.com, p12b
Sv Svetlana/Shutterstock.com, p13r WR studio/Shutterstock.com, p17b roibu/
Shutterstock.com, p21b WR studio/Shutterstock.com, p24 Petr Toman/Shutterstock.
com, p25bl Funk Dooby via www.flickr.com, p25br Phunkt via www.flickr.com, p26 J.A.
Dunbar/Shutterstock.com, p27 Jack Zarzycki/raysmtb.com, p29l Pavel Burchenko/
Shutterstock.com, p30t Maxim Petrichuk/Shutterstock.com, p30bl Steve Bennett via
Wikimedia Commons, p30br LiveMedia/Shutterstock.com.

Disclaimer
Every effort has been made to contact copyright holders of any material reproduced
in this book. Any omissions will be rectified in subsequent printings if notice is given
to the publisher.

A catalogue record for this
book is available from the
National Library of Australia

CONTENTS

WOW!

EPIC ADVENTURE AWAITS!

WHAT IS MOUNTAIN BIKING?

Mountain biking is not for the faint-hearted. It involves riding off-road over challenging terrain on a specially designed bicycle. Bomb down purpose-built trails, leap over dirt jumps and navigate tricky rock gardens using core balance, endurance and epic bike handling skills.

NEED MORE REASONS TO RIDE?

Mountain biking is great for fitness and mental well-being! It's an amazing workout that's great for your cardio fitness and helps to build strength and stamina. Not only does it reduce stress and sharpen your reflexes, but it's super extreme fun! Why wouldn't you?

TALK ABOUT DETERMINATION!

In 2014, Gavin Godfrey accomplished the very first jaw-dropping triple backflip on a mountain bike!

BRIEF HISTORY

The first bicycle was invented in 1817, but real mountain biking made its official debut around the early 1970s in the USA. It grew in popularity in the 1980s, taking the world by storm as mass media began broadcasting the big riding events. Today, the mountain bike industry is booming! It is now an exciting, mainstream adventure activity, but be warned – it's highly addictive!

TIMELINE

1817 The first steerable bicycle was invented by Karl Drais. It had no pedals and a wooden plank as a seat. He called it the Swiftwalker since it was meant to assist fast walking.

EARLY 1970s

Cyclists in and around Marin County in the USA started assembling Clunkers. These salvaged paper-boy bikes from the 1930s and '40s could be used to bomb down bush paths and bumpy fire trails.

FUN FACT

The Swiftwalker bike design is still popular today! It's now known as a balance bike and is popular with very young riders.

1976 Clunker enthusiasts began competing in a series of off-road downhill races, where the riders could skid through 52 hair-raising turns.

1977 Joe Breeze constructed the world's first purpose-built mountain bike

1980s Specialized Bicycle Components became the first company to begin mass producing and distributing the famous Stumpjumper bike – the very first in its category.

1996 Mountain biking was featured at the Atlanta Olympic Games.

2000 Mountain biking became a popular adventure sport, with a range of specialised bikes becoming available in bike shops.

2010 Public demand drives an increase in highly specialised mountain bikes and a series of carefully engineered mountain bike trails.

2020 Mountain biking becomes so popular during a global pandemic, that many shops sell out of bikes!!

SOLD OUT!

WHERE DO PEOPLE RIDE?

Mountain bike parks and trails are available all over the world. Contractors, clubs, park rangers and volunteers work together to set up and maintain purpose-built mountain bike trails for everyone to enjoy.

COOL STUFF

IN SEARCH OF THE ULTIMATE ADRENALINE RUSH?

The world's longest mountain bike descent is in the Annapurna region of Nepal. It takes three days to ride the epic trail which descends through a whopping 4,530 metres!

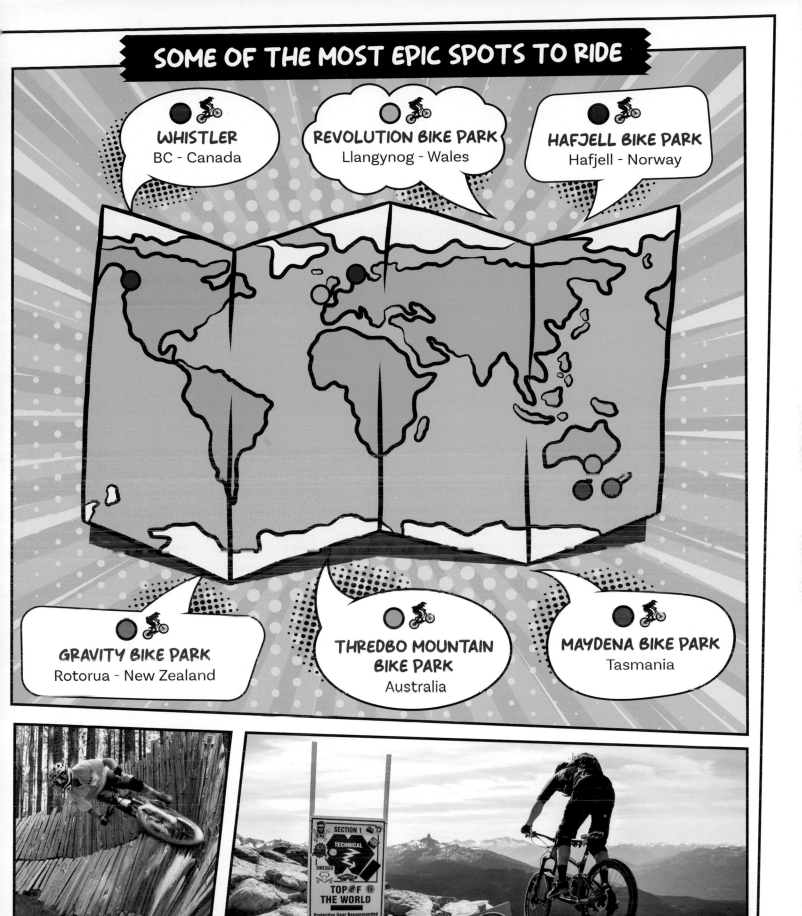

LEARNING TO RIDE

Riding a bike is easy enough right, but are you ready for more adrenaline?

If speeding down rough, rocky, uneven terrain is more your thing, staying upright can become a real and exciting challenge. From the technical bits to the fast, fun, strenuous, nerve-wracking and terrifying bits, there's a lot to learn!

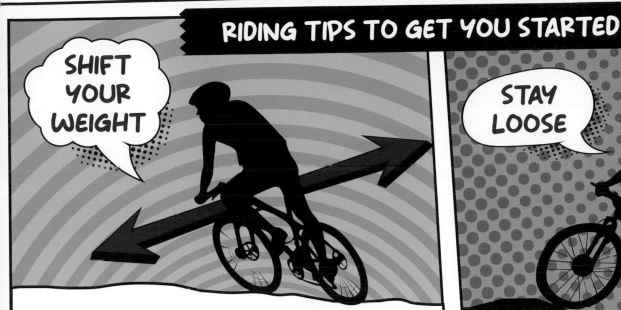

SHIFT YOUR WEIGHT

Shifting your weight from one side to another, or from front to back will shift your centre of gravity. This is important. Leaning your body's weight on your bike increases a friendly force called torque. It's this downward force that helps you sail expertly around corners, power efficiently up hills, bomb safely down hills and stylishly hop through boulder sections, jumps and everything in between.

STAY LOOSE

When bombing down a trail, you want to flow with your bike rather than fight with it. Keep your body loose but poised. Keep your arms and legs bent, ready to spring into action.

COMMIT

One of the single most important challenges when mountain biking is to commit to the challenge. Trust in the path that you have chosen and don't hold back. It can feel scary at first, but your confidence will improve the more you do it and your riding skills will progress light years ahead.

MAINTAIN MOMENTUM

Even though it's scary, speed is your friend. It will help you sail smoothly over tricky terrain and keep you moving forward. Have you noticed that it's harder to stay upright when you're going super slow on flat, level ground? The same is true when the terrain gets gnarly; it just hurts more if you fall – so keep it moving!

DISCIPLINES WITHIN THE SPORT

All mountain biking requires core strength, epic bike handling skills, balance and lightning fast reactions, but there is a huge variety of disciplines within this diverse sport.

CROSS COUNTRY

This is the most common style of mountain biking. It's accessible to all skill levels and involves a variety of features. Typically, a rider can expect to be riding on single-tracks, fire roads, dirt trails and even gravel. Riders will navigate steep climbs and descents, rock gardens and fun drops.

EPIC! Downhill trails are all downhill!

DOWNHILL

Riders usually catch a shuttle or a ski lift to the trailhead then zoom down the course over exhilarating jumps, obstacle rollovers and massive drops. This is one of the most thrilling and risky disciplines in mountain biking.

DIRT JUMPING

Most trails have a few dirt jumps built into them, but dirt jumping parks are a whole new level of extreme! There's a wide range of ramps and jumps at various heights. If you're a courageous daredevil, you can take your ride to mind-blowing new heights with perfectly engineered ramps that angle experienced riders into perfect flips!

FREERIDE

Freeriding is about having fun and finding the most creative path possible.

The rider can include gravity-defying aerial manoeuvres, stylish navigation of technical trail features, catching air and landing jumps. Freeriding is about creating cool, personalised lines over any terrain.

WOW!
Freeriding uses style and skill!

WHAT IS ROAD CYCLING?

Just as the name suggests, road cycling takes place on sealed roads with a purpose-built bicycle. It's not mountain biking, but it is an excellent way to go fast, go far and immerse yourself in cycling.

Not only does road cycling have awesome health benefits, but it also requires focus, determination and strength to go the distance and make it up those monster climbs.

ROAD BIKES VS MOUNTAIN BIKES

A road bike is lightweight, efficient and engineered for maximum performance on a smooth surface. It has narrow tyres and, usually, special 'drop' handlebars that put the rider in an aggressive, forward-leaning position. This improves aerodynamics which helps them go faster, stay upright and ride in a steady, usually straight, direction.

Mountain bikes are designed to handle rough terrains like dirt, mud, snow and gravel. They have strong, thick frames and thick knobbly tyres. They have special components that are essential to protect the bike and its rider from the extra punishments that off-road riding deals out.

ROAD BIKE

MOUNTAIN BIKE

VS

COOL STUFF

TOUR DE FRANCE

The Tour De France is an annual men's bicycle race held over 23 days. The race has 21 stages and runs mainly through France but also passes through other nearby countries.

WHAT ABOUT BMX?

BMX is short for bicycle motocross

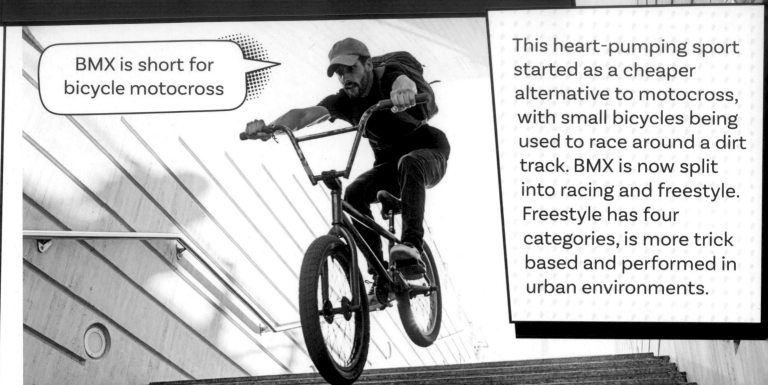

This heart-pumping sport started as a cheaper alternative to motocross, with small bicycles being used to race around a dirt track. BMX is now split into racing and freestyle. Freestyle has four categories, is more trick based and performed in urban environments.

PARK

Park riding is mostly at skateparks, riding transitions like half-pipes, box jumps and spines.

STREET

Riders find unique features in their urban landscape like stairs, curbs and handrails to pull off tricks such as manuals – like a wheelie, but without pedalling, tail whips – where the back of the bike spins around the stationary front wheel, and full spins.

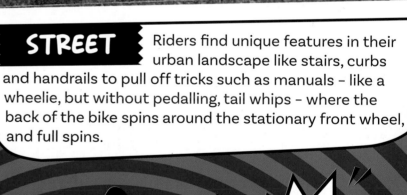

WOW!
Street riding is the most popular style of BMX!

FLATLAND

DIRT

Dirt riding is usually on a special track that has been purpose-built with tabletop jumps, berms, rollers and more. These tracks can range from years of sculpted works of dirt-art to a few small piles of soil in a vacant lot.

This impressive style was inspired by riders who didn't have many features to ride in their area. Tricks are performed on flat ground and require extreme balance and control. It's one of the more challenging BMX disciplines.

COOL STUFF

BMX Racing made its way to the Olympics in 2008 but BMX Freestyle made its official debut in the Tokyo 2020 Games.

MOUNTAIN BIKE PARTS

Mountain bikes have special components that allow their riders to go where road riders can't. Tougher, bigger and knobblier tyres are just the start!

1. SHOCKS

There are two styles of mountain bike – hardtail and dual-suspension. A hardtail bike is great for smoother, faster trails and only has suspension on the front forks. A dual-suspension bike has additional suspension at the rear to make technical trail riding much easier and more fun.

2. DROP POSTS

Mountain bike riders need to change the height of their seat quickly and often – unlike road riders. A drop post can shoot the (usually wider and more padded) seat up or down at the flick of a switch to avoid serious damage to sensitive body parts!

3. GEARS

Mountain bike gears are specifically designed for spreading force evenly – unlike road bikes which are all about speed. Ever feel like your legs are going to fall off riding up a massive hill? Gears make it easier to keep a steady pedalling speed, or cadence. They provide better rider control whether you're sweating the uphill or bombing a sweet downhill.

HOW DO GEARS WORK?

GEAR HUB

CHAINRING

Pedalling a bike turns a chainring – which is a cogwheel. A notched chain connects this cogwheel to the gear hub on the bike's back axle. A gear hub is a group of different sized cogwheels that can turn the back wheel at different speeds.

Some mountain bikes have up to three different sized chainrings, but modern bikes often only have one. This reduces the chance of a slipped chain when changing between cogs. Bikes with more chainrings have more gear options but need a front derailleur. This makes hills easier and flats faster, but the extra components can cause issues on more technical trails.

LOW GEAR

Smaller distance covered but more power generated

Pedalling on a larger cog - or a low gear – is easier and really helps on the steep hills!

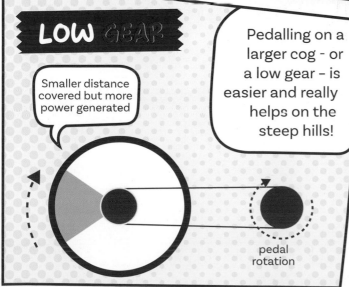

pedal rotation

HIGH GEAR

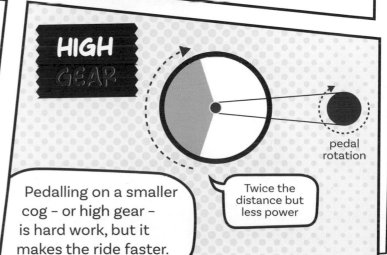

pedal rotation

Twice the distance but less power

Pedalling on a smaller cog – or high gear – is hard work, but it makes the ride faster.

ELECTRIC BIKES

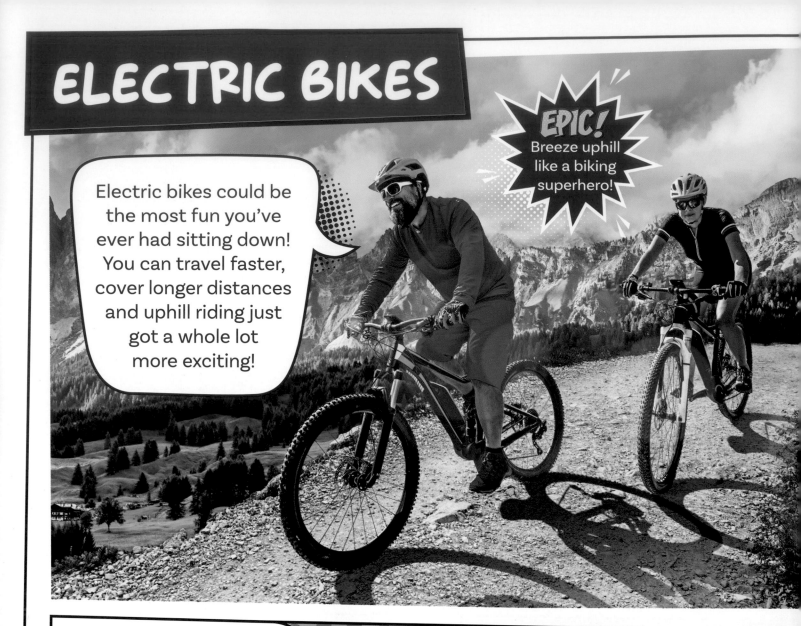

Electric bikes could be the most fun you've ever had sitting down! You can travel faster, cover longer distances and uphill riding just got a whole lot more exciting!

EPIC! Breeze uphill like a biking superhero!

An e-bike has an electric motor that is fed from a battery mounted on its frame. Some e-bikes have a throttle similar to a motorbike, so you can stop pedalling altogether! Other bikes have pedal assist where you still have to pedal but the motor kicks in when you do - making it a much easier ride.

The battery pack is mounted on the frame of the bike

The throttle or bike computer is usually on the handlebars

SHUTTLES AND LIFTS

Believe it or not, there are some riders who are just natural-born hill climbers. For the rest of us, there's shuttles and even ski lifts! Shuttle services are provided at most mountain bike parks. This can be a bus or car that transports mountain bike riders and their bikes to the top of a trail – so they only need to do the fun ride down.

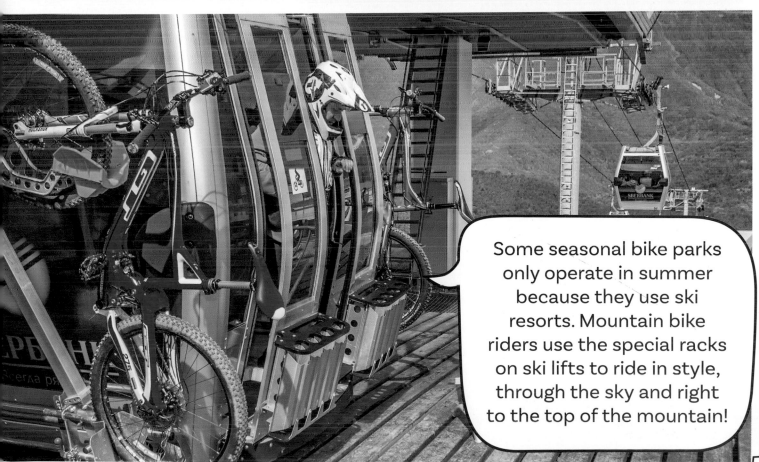

Some seasonal bike parks only operate in summer because they use ski resorts. Mountain bike riders use the special racks on ski lifts to ride in style, through the sky and right to the top of the mountain!

EXTRA EQUIPMENT AND CLOTHING

There is an endless list of gear and accessories to pick up if you're going to become a mountain bike rider, but here are the basics to get you started – after you have the bike of course!

CLOTHING

Mountain bike clothing needs to be breathable, flexible and tough. You will work hard, sweat a lot, need to move around and could even come off your bike. Your clothing needs to keep you comfortable and be able to take a beating!

GLOVES

Gloves protect your hands against scrapes and scratches but also prevent falls in the first place. They soak up your hard-earned sweat and give you greater handlebar control and feedback from the bike. Gloves – and good footwear – are the essential connection between human and machine.

BODY ARMOUR

HELMET – OBVIOUSLY!
This is the most important piece of equipment you will own as a mountain bike rider. A full-face helmet is best for rocky or otherwise gnarly trails because it protects the face, chin and mouth as well as the head.

KNEE AND ELBOW PADS
No, these aren't just for beginners! Professional riders use this essential gear for a reason.

EXTRAS

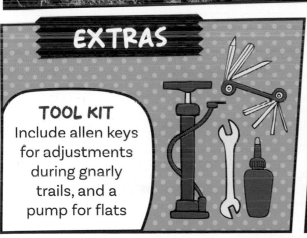

TOOL KIT
Include allen keys for adjustments during gnarly trails, and a pump for flats

HYDRATION
Never underestimate how much this can affect your enjoyment of a rad ride!

POWER SNACK
for more power! Obviously ...

ENERGY LOW SUGAR BAR
ENERGY LOW SUGAR BAR
Peanut

FIRST AID KIT
Stacks happen! At the very least, have a basic kit with some band-aids, bandages and alcohol wipes. A space blanket can be a lightweight lifesaver.

TRAILS MAP
dont get lost in the woods

NAVIGATION
Phone GPS, a trail app with routes and mapping, or a paper map and great orienteering skills are a must. Getting lost can ruin an otherwise awesome day out!

PROFESSIONAL MOUNTAIN BIKERS

NINO SCHURTER

BORN: 13.05.1986

This Swiss rider boasts a jaw-dropping 40 World Cup Cross Country wins with 23 Podium finishes. Schurter has been at the top of his game for the last decade. He won Silver in the 2012 Olympics and took out the Gold medal in 2016.

RACHEL ATHERTON

BORN: 06.12.1987

Rachel Laura Atherton began riding BMX at the age of 8 and mountain biking at the age of 11. She is now a professional British downhill mountain bike racer with a mind-bending record number of 39 World Cup Downhill wins.

DANNY MACASKILL

BORN: 23.12.1985

Danny MacAskill is a Scottish mountain bike trials professional. Trials are where the rider has to complete an obstacle course without touching their feet to the ground. This style of riding is extremely skilful and demands expert control. Danny's videos have a viral success of over 500 million views on YouTube alone.

JILL KINTNER

BORN: 24.10.1981

Jill Kintner is a professional American BMX and Mountain Cross rider. She has a diverse set of skills including pump track, dual slalom, downhill, and speed and style – the question is "What can't she do?"

INDOOR RIDING

Imagine riding all day, rain, hail or shine. Well, some amazing bike enthusiasts have made this dream a reality!

HOW DOES IT WORK?

Indoor purpose-built tracks offer trails for beginners through to intermediate and advanced riders. The track is built mostly from wood and winds around inside a warehouse with many twists and turns. There are various features such as drop-offs, ramps, embankments and berms. Trails include natural surfaces with rocks and logs for authentic riding, so you can really up your skills.

ANYTHING LOOSE OR BROKEN? TELL THE FRONT DESK.

NOT SURE YOU CAN RIDE THE TRAIL? WALK IT FIRST.

PLEASE DON'T RIDE TRAILS BACK-WARDS.

EPIC! Check out Ray's MTN Bike Park

WHY RIDE INDOORS?

Indoor mountain bike parks can make you a better rider, because you can practise your jumps, cornering, pumping and bike handling skills in a safe, organised space. To 'session' is to repeatedly attempt trail sections until you've perfected them. Is there an indoor park near you? Why not crank some session time, so you can tear it up like a boss out on the trails!

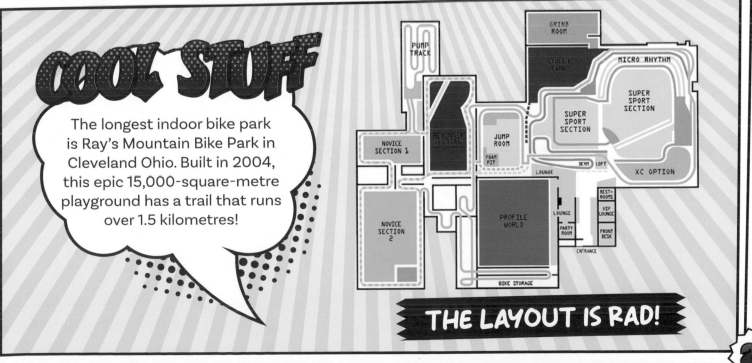

COOL STUFF

The longest indoor bike park is Ray's Mountain Bike Park in Cleveland Ohio. Built in 2004, this epic 15,000-square-metre playground has a trail that runs over 1.5 kilometres!

THE LAYOUT IS RAD!

Mountain biking is an extreme sport that comes with a high risk of injury – so be prepared!

A full-face helmet, gloves and body armour can make all the difference if you want to ride another day.

Be sure to keep your gear in tip-top condition and it will return the favour by looking after you. Remember, the wilderness is wild! Don't get caught out without human supplies – food, water, first aid, map and weather protection such as sunscreen or a raincoat.

COMING OFF YOUR BIKE

When riders come off, it can be full-on. Most of the time, your hands go down first, then your head. You can break a wrist, arm or even your face! Head injuries are dead serious. Seriously.

JUMPS

Know your limits!! Jumps can be small gently sloping mounds of dirt or almost vertical launch ramps that'll just about send you into orbit. Confidence and commitment are essential to make any jump. Trust the path you choose ... But beware; overconfident riders who make silly choices can regret it. Don't cave in to peer pressure. Build your skills steadily and only jump the jumps when you're ready to choose the right line for you. Jumps can be easy to misjudge and tricky to land, so get to know your limits gradually.

LOOSE TERRAIN

Mountain bike terrain almost always involves rough, loose or rocky sections. It's up to you to master your bike handling skills to stay safe. It's common to come away from a ride with a few extra bruises and some scratches, but usually it's totally worth it!

MTB RIDING EVENTS

From amateur cross country challenges to high profile downhill racing, there is something for everyone in the mountain biking world.

Some of the most exciting competitions held include:

THE MTB WORLD CUP

ENDURO WORLD SERIES

SUMMER OLYMPICS

GLOSSARY

AERIAL MANOEUVRES	tricks performed mid-air
AERODYNAMICS	the way air flows around an object with the least resistance
AMATEUR	participation without payment – just for fun!
BERMS	raised corners of a trail that raise the rider horizontally
BOMBING	travelling downhill at high speed
BOX JUMP	box-shaped jump obstacles in bike parks
CADENCE	the number of pedal revolutions per minute
CARDIO	cardiovascular and heart health
CENTRE OF GRAVITY	the point where the mass of the body is concentrated
CHAINRINGS	cogs attached to the pedal axle of a bike
COG	wheel with metal 'teeth' that interact with a notched chain
DROP-OFF	sudden edge with a sharp vertical descent on a trail
DUAL SLALOM	set of two identical racecourses where riders compete simultaneously
DUAL-SUSPENSION	type of bike with both front and rear suspension components
E-BIKE	bike with an electrically charged motor that assists with pedal power
ENDURANCE	performance under harsh conditions or against exhaustion
HARDTAIL	type of bike with only front suspension, no rear suspension
LINE	imaginary 'path' that riders plan and follow
MANUAL	rolling on the back wheel, without pedalling
PUMP TRACK	track that can be ridden without pedalling, using body bouncing
QUARTERPIPE	smooth-surfaced wall with a curved base used for performing stunts
ROLLOVER	obstacle that can be navigated by free-wheeling across it
SESSION	repeated attempts at a trail section, to master a particular skill
SHUTTLE	special minibus service for transporting bikes and riders to trail tops
SPINE	double-sided jump ramp, without a tabletop or gap
TAIL WHIP	BMX trick where the bike whips around its stationary front wheel
TERRAIN	type of ground
TRAILHEAD	top of the trail
TRANSITIONS	control of sudden changes between terrain or obstacle types

INDEX